Understanding Horses with

Caddie

Carola von Kessel

Illustrations by
Irmtraud Guhe

Contents

Imprint

Copyright © 2004 by
Cadmos Verlag GmbH, Brunsbek
Project management: Editmaster Co Ltd, Northampton
Translated by: Claire Williams
Design and setting: Ravenstein, Verden
Illustrations: Irmtraud Guhe
Printed by Grindeldruck, Hamburg

Printed in the EU

ISBN 3-86127-948-7

Jacky & Caddie

Welcome to *Caddie's* Equine Academy!

Hi, my name is *Caddie*. Together with my young owner Jacky, I'm going to teach you how to understand what your horse is saying.

But how can you do that – understand what we horses are saying? First of all of course you will need to learn our language. You need to know how to read our body language and learn to tell what our facial expressions mean. You will also need to know all about our basic needs and behaviour.

This book is a language course for anyone who would like to understand their horse better. And so that learning is more fun, Jacky and I have worked out a few puzzles for you to test your knowledge on.

Have fun reading and learning your horse's language!

Best wishes,

Caddie

How horses live

United they stand

Horses are herd animals. The other members of the herd
or their stable mates are like family to them. In the herd,
they feel cared for and safe.

*One horse will always stand watch and will warn
the other herd members of any danger.*

Obvious hierarchy

Every group of horses has rules that must be followed. The hierarchy governs
each horse's position within the herd. The leader is usually an older, experienced
horse. This horse has special rights, such as being first to food when the horses
are all fed together. But the leader (who may be male or female) also has the
most responsibilities and must take care that the other members of the herd feel
protected.
It is common, for example, that you will see nearly all horses sleeping in a field
while the leader stands watch.

If a horse has a lower ranking (here, the horse with the darker mane) he must always give way to his herd mates.

Horses that are ranked lower have less power and for example must always move out of the way when a higher-ranked horse approaches him. On the plus side, lower-ranked horses have fewer responsibilities and can always be certain that their leader will look after them.

Caddie's Horse sense

Horse watching

You can learn a lot about us horses by spending time watching us in the field. You will see that some horses immediately move out of the way of certain other horses when they approach. The horses that get out of the way quickly have a lower ranking in the herd. They know that they will be in big trouble if they get in the way of a higher ranked horse. As we are peace-loving animals, we'd rather move aside than cause trouble.

Always at the ready!

Horses are naturally very cautious. Unlike predators – animals that hunt, such as cats and dogs – horses are animals of flight; in other words, when danger threatens, they run away.

Horses living in the wild must always be prepared for a predator to appear and attack them. Even though there are no lions or tigers roaming our fields, a horse's instinct to flee is deeply ingrained in them.

Because horses are animals of flight, they are easily frightened by new things or by sudden movements.

Jacky's Tip: Shying is OK!

If a horse sees something new or unusual, he will often shy. This is what you call it when he suddenly jumps to one side or stops abruptly. From a horse's viewpoint, shying is the clever thing to do: in the wild, a horse that doesn't move out of the way of danger quickly enough is soon going to be eaten by his predators. That's why you should never punish a shying horse. Instead you should try to remain calm and relaxed. This will show your horse that there is nothing to be afraid of. Speak to him quietly and breathe deeply and regularly. This will help your horse to relax as well.

Favourite hobby: Eating

Horses are herbivores. In the wild they spend their whole day looking for grass, herbs, bark, foliage and twigs.

A horse's senses

Horses can smell a lot of things that we humans are not even aware of. Their sight is also different to ours: because they can see in almost all directions, they can see objects and movements behind them at an angle without even having to turn their head. If they drop their head, they can see only a few metres in front. With a lifted head however they can see far into the distance.

Their mobile ears pick up noises from all different directions. In addition horses have a well-developed sense of touch and can sense the softest of touches on their skin – think of a horse twitching his skin when a fly lands on him.

Around their mouth and nostrils they have long whiskers with which they can feel things.

Horses feel with their whiskers like we do with our fingers.

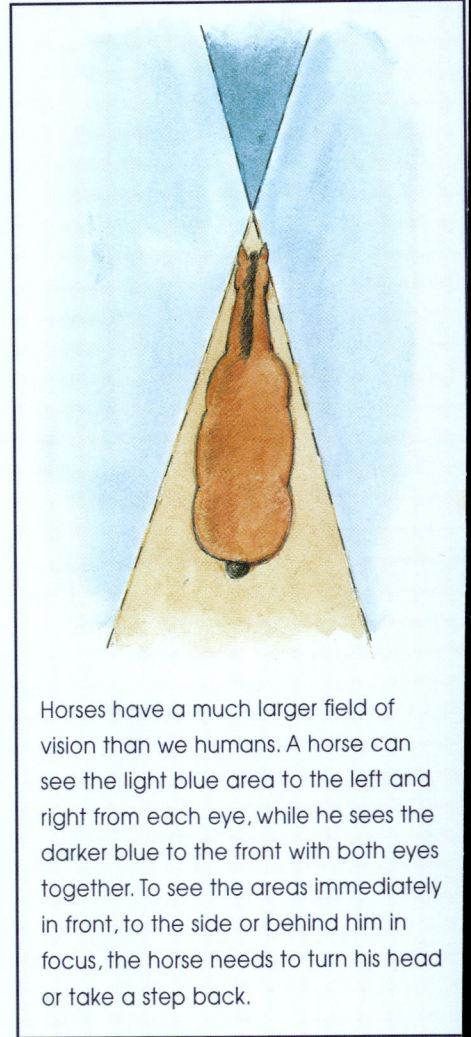

Horses have a much larger field of vision than we humans. A horse can see the light blue area to the left and right from each eye, while he sees the darker blue to the front with both eyes together. To see the areas immediately in front, to the side or behind him in focus, the horse needs to turn his head or take a step back.

These horses can decide for themselves whether they stay outside or go into the field shelter. This is much more natural for horses than being kept in individual stables.

Caddie's Horse Sense

Happiness is ...

We horses prefer to be outside and to feel the snow, rain, sun and wind on our backs.

So that we stay healthy and don't get bored, we need lots of exercise and the company of other horses. In addition it's important that we get a constant supply of feed throughout the day.

When we are stabled permanently we really don't feel at our best. It is much nicer if we can choose whether to be under cover or outside. Being turned out somewhere with natural shelter or access to a field shelter meets our needs best of all.

How horses communicate

Talking faces

Horses show their feelings with their ears, eyes, nostrils, and muzzle as well as through other types of body language.

Because they can combine a variety of postures and facial expressions you need some experience to correctly understand their mood.

The horse on the right is friendly and in a good mood. You can see this from his pricked ears and the interested expression on his face.

A horse feeling pain looks at first glance similar to a horse that is feeling tired. If you observe horses carefully you will be able to read their expressions more accurately.

This horse is listening to something behind him – his ears turned to point backwards give this away.

Jacky's Tip:

Understanding horses!

In order to understand your horse's mood you should always look at the whole horse, not just the different parts of him individually. If a horse lays his ears back, for example, it's not necessarily a sign that he is in a bad mood. When a horse is dozing or listening to noises behind him, his ears may also be pointed backwards. Pricked ears can also mean different things – curiosity, enjoyment or excitement. And when a horse swishes his tail he may be in a bad mood but he may also just be trying to get rid of a few pesky flies! It's the combination of facial expression, ears and the body language that will tell you how a horse is really feeling.

A horse's voice

Horses neigh with an open mouth.

I'm sure you've already heard a horse neigh. But what is a horse saying when he neighs? If a horse neighs loudly and shrilly he is trying to get the attention of other horses. To greet you or another horse, on the other hand, he will nicker in a low "bubbling" tone.

This sounds similar to the sound when he's happy to see you because you are bringing him his dinner. Mares use a similar sound when they wicker to their foals in a low calming tone.

Snorting and groaning

If a horse is standing relaxed and blows gently through his nose at length, he is showing that he is feeling well. If on the other hand he snorts strongly in short bursts then he is excited or is scared of something.

Quiet groaning can also be a sign of relaxed well-being, but if a horse is groaning in bursts or is straining, then he is probably in pain. Some horses will also groan loudly in protest, for example when they are being asked to do things they don't want to do.

This picture shows an excited horse with raised head. His nostrils are flared and his ears pricked.

Caddie's Horse Sense

Talk to us!

We horses can learn to respond to your voice commands. The tone of your voice is very important though – if you want to calm us down you should speak in a low tone and draw out or lengthen the words. On the other hand if you would like a horse to go faster, you need to raise the tone of your voice higher and sound more encouraging. Find out what voice commands the horse you ride has learnt and responds to. It helps us if all humans use the same words in the same way.

13

Caddie's
Home

Enter the solutions to the questions in the circles. When you enter all the letters from the rings numbered 1–12 into the gaps at the bottom of the next page you will learn where Caddie goes when the weather gets bad.

The solution can be found on page 30.

1. What do you call it when a horse uses his voice?

◯ ◯ ◯ ◯ ◯ ◯ ◯ ◯
　　2

2. What do horses use to feel with instead of fingers?

◯ ◯ ◯ ◯ ◯ ◯ ◯ ◯
　　　　　　8

3. What do you call a baby horse?

◯ ◯ ◯ ◯
　　4

4. What is the main activity of a horse when living out or in the wild?

◯ ◯ ◯ ◯ ◯ ◯
3

5. Which instinct is the reason why horses run away at the first sign of danger?

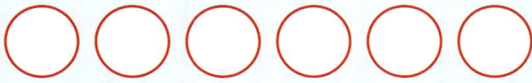

◯ ◯ ◯ ◯ ◯ ◯
1   10

6. What do you call it when a horse is taken by surprise and suddenly jumps to the side?

◯ ◯ ◯ ◯ ◯ ◯
6

7. What do horses mostly eat in the field?

◯ ◯ ◯ ◯ ◯
12

8. What do you call the highest ranked horse in a group of horses?

◯ ◯ ◯ ◯   ◯ ◯ ◯ ◯ ◯ ◯
       9   5

9. What do you call horse's feet?

◯ ◯ ◯ ◯ ◯ ◯
7   11

Where does Caddie go when the weather gets bad?

◯ ◯ ◯ ◯ ◯ ◯ ◯ ◯ ◯ ◯ ◯ ◯
1 2 3 4 5   6 7 8 9 10 11 12

The **Basics** of horse language

Stay relaxed

Horses will often stand with lowered head in the field or stable. Their ears will droop to each side or to the back, they will gaze into the distance at nothing and their lower lip will droop.

Horses will often also rest a hind leg, and the tail will hang relaxed.

In this position horses are at their most relaxed.

When horses are dozing they will usually rest a hind leg. The lowered head and the laid back ears show that this horse is relaxed.

Jacky's Tip:

Hello, I'm here!

Before you approach a new horse you should speak to him quietly, so that he notices that you are there. If you don't make him aware of you, he may be surprised when you suddenly touch him.

Only touch him when he turns his head towards you. Then you can be certain that he has noticed you.

Hello!
Who are you?

This is how horses greet each other.
The smell tells them who the other one is.

Horses will often sniff and blow into each other's nostrils as a greeting. The smell tells them a lot about each other. If a horse is sniffing around you with pricked ears he is only trying to find out who you are.

Foals show adult horses that they are small and need protecting by this chewing or mouthing movement.

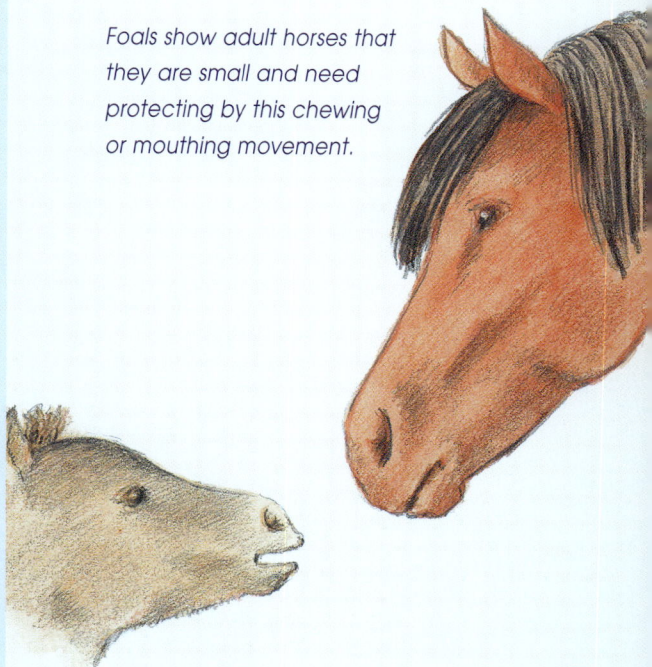

Please don't hurt me!

Young horses especially will make a chewing movement with their mouth when they meet other horses although they are not eating at all. This means in horse language "I'm small and harmless – please don't hurt me!"

Attention Everyone!

A horse that is looking in a particular direction with a raised head and pricked ears has seen something interesting.

He may snort excitedly and begin to prance about or swish his tail nervously. In such a case you should expect him to suddenly take off – either to examine whatever he has seen more closely or to get himself away to safety. It may also be that the horse suddenly races off.

That's why you should always watch out and be careful that you don't get in his way.

This horse has seen something: his whole body is tense and his head is lifted high.

Caddie's horse sense

Quietly does it!

By now you will have learnt that our tendency to be easily startled has a purpose: It helps to keep us out of danger. So that you don't scare or startle us by mistake, you should always stay calm around us. Loud shrieking or sudden movements make us nervous – and you don't want that, do you?

For goodness sake!

A horse will also hold his head high when he is startled to get a better view of the potential danger. His eyes will widen in fear and his ears will flicker back and forth nervously. The horse will often jump to the side, or run off.

Trouble and strife!

Be careful – take this horse seriously. His flattened ears, pinched nostrils and his head stretched out shows that he is annoyed.

Horses are usually peaceful animals. Serious fights are rare, but despite this horses can still get annoyed – for example by irritating herd mates or incompetent humans. If a horse lays his ears back flat, moves his head forwards jerkily and small wrinkles form around his mouth and nostrils then he should be taken seriously – he's not kidding. He might even bare his teeth. Be careful – this horse is angry and could strike out.

This horse is annoyed as well: he has laid back ears, is swishing his tail and is threatening to kick with his hind leg.

Warning from behind

You should also watch out if a horse suddenly turns his hindquarters towards you. Perhaps you are lucky and he'd just like to be scratched. It could also mean that he's going to kick you at any moment.

19

Jacky's Tip: Be safe, not sorry

Horses can't see what is happening directly behind them. If they are suddenly aware of a movement or noise, they may be startled and lash out behind. A kick would land you in hospital in the blink of an eye. That's why you should always watch out when you are walking behind horses. The same also applies if you are standing in front of a horse. Just imagine if the horse takes fright and takes off suddenly over the top of you ...

Rubbing and scratching

Some horses try to rub themselves against you. Even if you enjoy him wanting to be close to you and don't mind him doing this, you shouldn't allow him to do this. This is because it shows that your horse doesn't respect you. No horse would dare to try rubbing himself against a higher-ranking member of his herd. If it happens,
simply push his head away and say "no" loudly and firmly.

If a horse tries to use you as a scratching post, he doesn't really respect you.

20

Jacky's Tip:

How to earn your horse's respect

To get your horse to respect and obey you, you will need to gain as much experience as possible. In the beginning it is quite normal for you to be scared or nervous of horses – after all, they are very large and strong! The longer you are around them though the more confident you will become. At some stage you will eventually realise that you understand them so well that you are able to assume a higher-ranking position than them. To get to this stage you must be very confident when around horses. You should not, for example, move aside when a horse wants to get past you. Instead the horse should give way to you – just as he would do in a herd when approached by a higher-ranking member.

Mutual Grooming

You will often see how two horses appear to use their teeth on each other's coats. This is actually a labour of friendship. The horses are scratching each other with their teeth because their skin or coat is itchy.

Companion horses will often scratch each other along the mane, on the back and on the croup – the rear end.

Caddie's   Horse Sense

Rolling is fun

When I'm itchy, I really enjoy rolling on the ground, most of all in sand. Horses that aren't turned out all the time are often allowed to have a roll after being ridden in the manège. Before we roll we check the ground by sniffing the surface thoroughly and turning in a small circle. Then we bend our front legs first, lie down and rub our head, neck, back and flanks on the ground.

By doing this we loosen any dirt and hair so that our skin won't be itchy any more. After rolling we stand up and shake ourselves thoroughly – it's a great feeling!

"Come and play with me!" Young horses especially love to play together in the field.

Horseplay

When out in the field, if a horse runs around another member of the herd, stands on his hind legs (that's called rearing) and tries to nip the other, then it's usually because he wants to play.

● ● ● ● ● ● ● ● ●

Serious fights between horses are very rare.

When it gets serious ...

Sometimes though there are serious arguments, especially when a new horse is introduced to an existing group. This is because a new ranking needs to be sorted out. Before a horse attacks another he will usually threaten to do so first (look back at page 19). Only when the other horse doesn't give in or back down will it come to a fight.
If two mares have a go at each other they usually turn their hindquarters to each other and kick out until one sur-renders. They will often squeal loudly during the fight.
When stallions fight it out they will rear and try to bite the other in the neck or shoulder.
Fights amongst horses are very dangerous as the defeated opponent can be seriously injured.

The Flehmen response

It looks really funny when a horse shows the "Flehmen" response. When he does it he will roll his top lip back and suck air into his mouth. This is usually a response to unusual smells, for example new or unknown horses.

When a horse does this he is rolling his top lip back to be better able to identify interesting smells.

Caddie's Horse sense

TLC for horses

Most horses enjoy being stroked or patted by people. I love it when Jacky scratches me along my mane. There are other horses though that aren't so keen on being touched, or that are ticklish in certain spots. Some horse owners don't like it when their horses are patted by others. Please always check with a horse's owner before you start to pat a strange horse.

Boy, am I tired!

When a relaxed horse suddenly opens his mouth wide and pulls up his top lip he is yawning – just like we do. When he does this you can see his tongue and down his throat.

Just as with us humans, horses sometimes yawn when they are tired or bored.

Dozing and sleeping

A horse can doze when standing up, resting one of his hind legs (look at page 16). When feeling safe, he will also lie down. Often a horse will doze when half lying down with his legs folded up underneath himself and with his head and neck held up. Horses can only really sleep deeply when they are lying out flat with their legs stretched out.

Horses will often doze in this position. If they want to sleep deeply then they will lie out flat on their sides.

When horses wind-suck they swallow air. Often habits like this form out of boredom.

Jacky's Tip:

Please don't let me get bored!

If a horse is standing around in a stable all day with little to do they sometimes develop behavioural problems, often called vices. Some rock from one leg to the other all day – back and forth, back and forth. This is known as weaving.

Other horses will bite into a fixed object such as the top of a stable door or the top rail of a fence and suck in air. This type of behaviour is called crib-biting and wind-sucking. Some horses will suck in and swallow air without fixing their teeth on anything. To get their minds on other things, horses showing signs of boredom should be turned out as much as possible.

Banging and pawing the ground

Many horses start to paw the ground with their front feet or will bang on the stable walls as soon as they see someone. They are doing this to get attention or are demanding feed. This behaviour is not only bad but can also be dangerous – horses can hurt themselves and others.
You should never praise a horse that is pawing or banging, either with words or feed! Otherwise he will think his behaviour has been successful and will do it all the more ...

Horses paw the ground for a number of different reasons. Perhaps he is begging for food, perhaps though he is about to lie down and is checking with his hooves whether the ground is suitable.

Caddie's Horse Sense

If you have read this far you will know how horses communicate. Knowing this you will understand us better. In addition, the language of horses is also the basis for all the commands that you give us. Please don't expect us to immediately understand you though. It takes a while until you can communicate with us properly. You will learn how you can use this when grooming or riding us in other Caddie-books.

27

I'm Bored!

How can you tell if a horse is bored?
When you take the letters from the
numbered boxes after completing all
the clues you will learn how to tell
when Caddie is tired.

Solution on page 30

Do you know these words?

1. What you enjoy doing with your horse.
2. Long hair at the horse's rear
3. What a horse does when he stands on his hind legs.
4. A sign of friendship between two horses.
5. Male horse
6. Unwanted begging with his front foot.
7. What mood a horse is in when he flattens his ears.
8. Another word for a horse's developed bad behaviour.
9. Behavioural problem when a horse swallows air.
10. Before a horse attacks, what will he do?
11. Position in which a horse can sleep deeply.
12. On the top of his head, a horse uses these to show his mood.

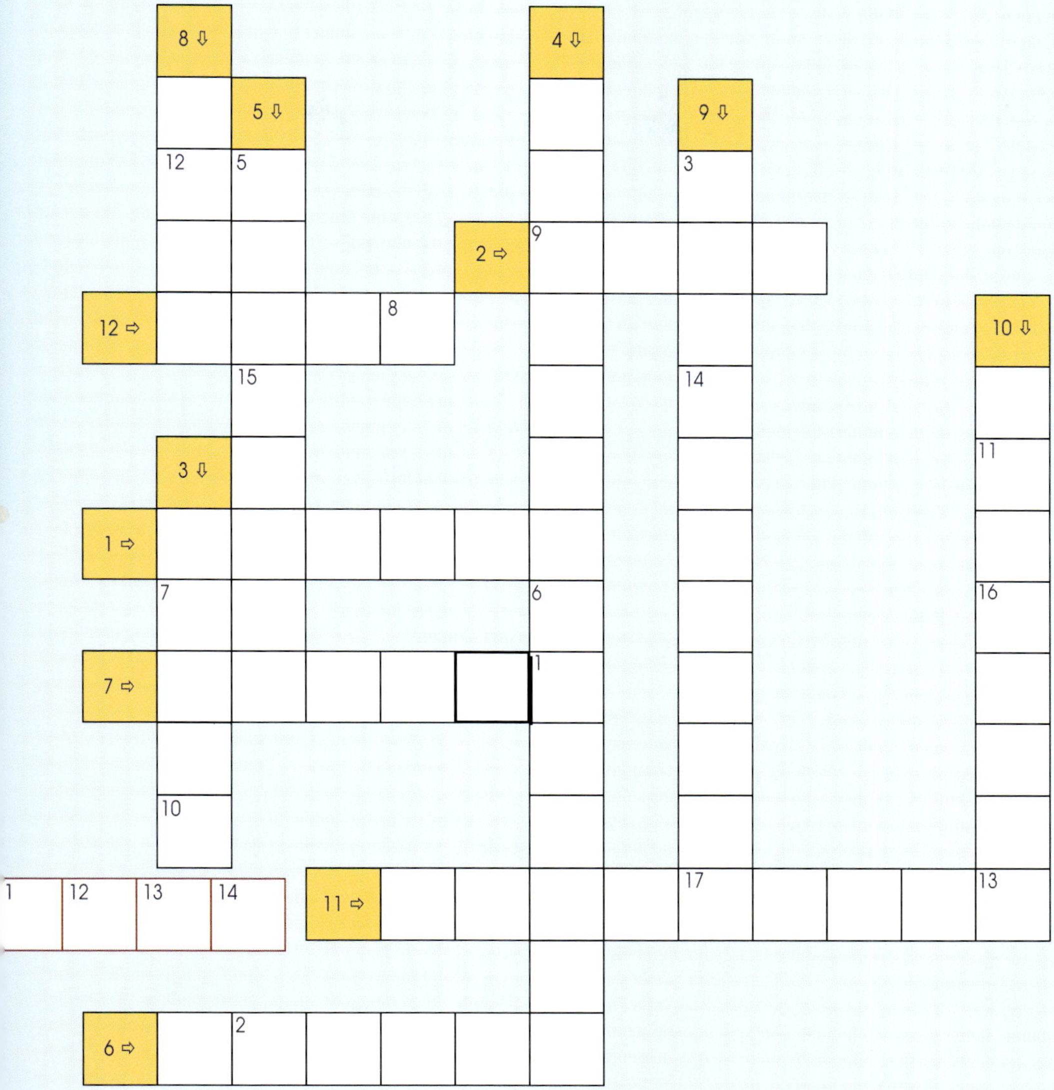

Hidden words:

When Caddie is tired he _ _ _ _ _ (1–5)

and _ _ _ _ _ (6–10) a _ _ _ _ _ _ _ (11–17)

Solutions

Solution
Page 14/15
The words we were looking
1. NEIGHING, 2. WHISKERS, 3. FOAL, 4. EATING, 5. FLIGHT,
6. SHYING, 7. GRASS, 8. HERD LEADER, 9. HOOVES.
When the weather gets bad Caddie goes to the **Field Shelter**.

Solution
page 28/29
"I'am bored"
The hidden words
are **Yawns and rests
a hindleg.**

Index

A/B

C

D/E

F

H

K/L

M/N

R/S

T

V/W

Y/Z

New

Caddie –
A new series of children's books for the young horse lover over 8 years old.

Get ready for a horse star of the extra special typ: Caddie, a brightly coloured representative of the horse world stars in a new series of books for children.

With a combination of illustrations and cartoons and well written text and puzzles this series is a well timed addition to literature aimed at a young audience of horse fans aged from 8 years old.

All Caddie books are illustrated in four-colour throughout: providing knowledge through fun at pocket money price.

Caddie

1

Hi there,
My name is Caddie. In this book I'm going to show you how to look after your horse properly. Plus fun puzzles all about horse care!

Carola von Kessel

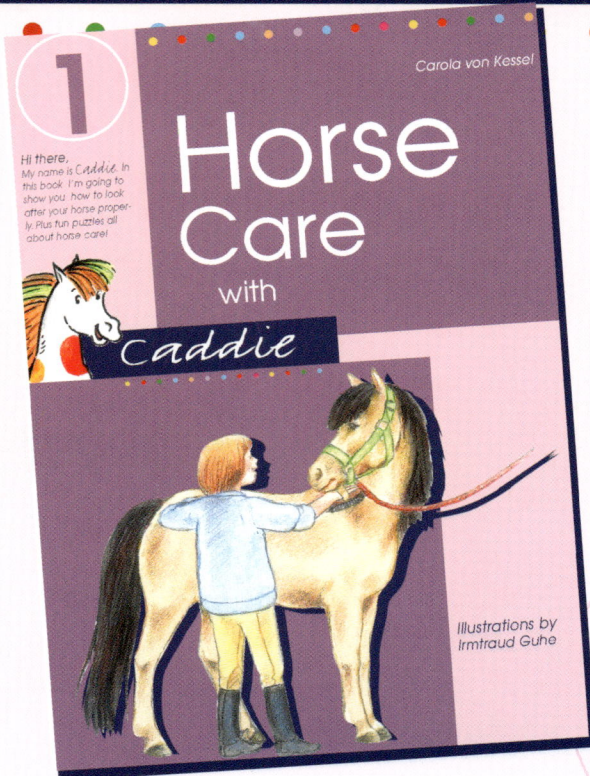

Horse Care with Caddie

Illustrations by Irmtraud Guhe

Horsecare with Caddie

Why do we groom horses?

What equipment do we need to do this properly and how do clean the coat, hooves, mane and tail?

This books gives clear and easy to follow answers and also provides plenty of information on safety when grooming.

ISBN 3-86127-949-5

£ 6,95